ADDICTIVE DEGREES OF TOLERANCE

For Drugs, Sex and Sin

CHARLES MWEWA

Published by:

ACP

Ottawa, ON Canada

www.acpress.ca

Email:

info@acpress.ca

ISBN: 978-1-998788-91-0

DEDICATION

To all those battling some kind of addictions.

CONTENTS

AUTHOR'S WORD

Humans have long understood that undesirable behaviors and habits have degrees of undesirability. This being so, though, there seems to be only one effect emanating from addictive behaviors, namely, offence. This effect comes in shades of increased or decreased tolerance. In this treatise, we treat only three of such addictive behaviors: Drugs, sex and sin.

DRUGS, SEX AND SIN

Drugs

A drug is either a medicine or a substance. It has a physiological effect especially when ingested or introduced into the body. Drugs have three characteristics: They have pleasant effects; and they are remedial in nature. But drugs can also be very addictive.

Pleasure Effect

Probably, this is the most common allure to drugs. The ecstasy and pleasure that drugs provide inform their use and desire. The so-called "high" effect draws in boys, girls, men and women a sense of excited satisfaction that they desire. It promises bliss and it may deliver.

Remedial Effect

Drugs heal or are the commonness healing source on earth. Without drugs, people, animals and plants cannot live long. It is drugs which single-handedly are responsible for extended longevity in human beings.

Addictive Effect

Pleasing and healing they are, but drugs are also very addictive. The Dictionary defines addiction as the fact or condition of being addicted to a particular substance, thing, or activity. Addiction is a danger because it is an abuse of the purpose for which something was intended. It has both psychological and physical consequences.

Thus, every drug has the potential to be addictive if misused or abused. Both misuse and abuse of drugs involve going beyond their limit to provide pleasure and healing. Once in an addictive mode, the victim loses control because of the effects of the drug. This loss of control can result in acts and behaviors that are antisocial, self-destructive and harmful.

Sex

Sex, like drugs, has three characteristic effects: Pleasurable; procreative; and it is addictive.

Pleasurable Effect

Sex is pleasant for the most part. The orgasmic reach is an awesome experience that humans desire. In being pleasant, sex relaxes human muscles and heightens chemical balances in the body and mind. It is also an important resource available to humans to function effectively and efficiently. Thus, sex is generally a very good human experience.

Procreative Effect

Without sex, there would be no human population. People are "made," so to speak, through sex. Therefore, sex was, is, and is going to be. Wherever humans are, there is sex and sexual intercourse. It is a rhythm of life. Sex should not be disparaged or cheapened, but sex shall always be there on earth.

Addictive Effect

Like drugs, sex is addictive. It can be abused and misused. When one is addicted to sex, sex ceases to be a thing of pleasure; it becomes a disease. It possesses the victim, derogates decency and erodes morals. The instrument of procreation and beauty becomes the weapon of shame and self-destruction. For the most part, prostitution and pornography are manifestations of abused, underused or misused sex. They are the result of, and not the cause of, sexual deviance and decay.

There are many factors to consider when dealing with sex addiction. These may include family upbringing and background, degree of early exposure to sexual products and activities, sexual abuse, child molestation, lack of guidance and lack of moral mentorship, exposure to pornography and pornographic materials, etc.

Others include wrong attitudes to sex, infidelity, promiscuity, unfulfilled marital sex, family splits, divorce, etc. However, all these factors have one thing in common, sex. It is a three-letter word but it can have three hundred deliberating effccts, if misplaced.

Sin

Like drugs and sex, sin is pleasant and addictive. It is even more; it can be offensive and burdensome.

Pleasant Effect

Sin heightens the senses. It promises uncommon pleasure and happiness. The danger of sin is that it corrupts morals and it is by design unlawful. It hits at the very core of social and spiritual orderliness.

Thus, it offends God and destroys social mores. It leads to waywardness and immorality. Allowed to persist, sin can erase the very foundation of social and spiritual order, and it can make humans fare worse than animals.

Sin destroys people as they destroy others. It is like a poison; it corrupts people and brings the entire human dignity into question. It is multiple dimensional and it can corrupt any virtue, manipulate it and turn it into a vice. It, basically, turns pleasure into prison. That is why it is abhorred by both gods and people. Government can crumble, businesses and marriages fail, and society becomes ungovernable where sin is tolerated. Sin reigns and the only thing that keeps it in check is God's grace.

Addictive Effect

 Sin is the most addictive behavior on earth. It's thus because it takes control of the entire sensual organism. It then invades the mind and the soul and it violates the body. It affects the total person - body, soul and spirit.

It may be very difficult to bring down without divine intervention. And what makes it even more ruthless and challenging is that its root is already resident in human nature. A person may desire to cease all sinful activities but she is powerless. Desire to stop alone is not enough. Sin possesses one and makes them its slave.

Burdensome

Sin is burdensome. It takes out the spirit of pleasure and leaves behind only its form. It forces one to do the very things that they hate. It is a mockery; it leads one through a mile only to ditch them halfway through. It rewards all actions with punishment, no matter how well the assignment was done. It betrays its own best interests and, in the end, it loses, taking with it as victims all those it enslaved.

Degrees of Tolerance

Drugs, sex and sin should be set within defined limits. Addiction comes because those who consume drug, sexual and sinful products exceed those limits.

Drugs

Drugs must be consumed within regulated limits. Exceeding those limits is not only dangerous to the health of the victim but it can lead to addiction. Addiction itself is a form of self-imposed disease. At some elevated exceedingly high levels of addiction, it becomes a disabling condition or a disorder. Rule of thumb, people must not trifle with drug regulations and governments must not relent to enforce regulated guidelines and laws on drugs.

Sex

Sex must be had within the confines of socially sanctioned parameters. The best place to enjoy sex is within legal marriage. Even within legal marriage, sex must be done within permitted and reasonable limits.

Abuse of sex can happen even in a marriage. Similarly, married couples should not stay unreasonably longer than what is necessary without sex. This will lead to infidelity and pornography. Couples are or will be to blame.

Sin

The limit set against sin is total abstinence. This is not because God requires it, but because of the inherently destructive nature of sin. A crime is committed against the entire society. Sin is committed against the entire world. A crime harms everyone; sin harms everything. That's why sin must be avoided, repented of and must be fled from.

When a sin happens, it must be confessed or restituted and completely stopped and never to be repeated. God's grace will suffice in times of great weakness.

Seven Principles of Tolerance

1. Limits exist to prolong pleasure and not to diminish it.
2. However pleasant something is, if abused, it reverts to displeasure, discomfort and dissatisfaction.
3. Even if poison may taste sweet, its inherent chemistry produces harm or death.
4. Addiction always happens when limits are being consistently broken.
5. Addiction erases the useful purpose of a thing and substitutes it with the wasteful effort of its opposite.
6. The burden created by the abuse and misuse of a thing is not removed by social or psychological or spiritual means, but by the combination of some or all of these.
7. The degree of tolerance of a thing is set by its purpose, but sin has no tolerable limits.

Conclusion

Drugs, sex and sin all give momentary relaxation and pleasure. Used as required or in moderation and for their attendant purpose, drugs and sex are panacea of insurmountable proportions in human sane objectivization. However, all the three, namely, drugs, sex and sin, are addictive and destructive if their use exceeds limits. Even a tiny amount of sin is injurious but too much of drugs and sex come to the same end. Drugs must only be used according to prescribed or regulated standards and guidelines; sex must be undertaken within the confines of a marriage without under- or overdoing it; and sin must not be allowed or tolerated.

Award-Winning, Best-Selling Author, Charles Mwewa (LLB; BA Law; BA Ed; LLM), is a prolific researcher, poet, novelist, lawyer, law professor and Christian apologist and intercessor. Mwewa has written no less than 100 books and counting in every genre and has exhibited his works at prestigious expos like the Ottawa International Book Expo and is the winner of the Coppa Awards for his signature publication, *Zambia: Struggles of My People.*
Mwewa and his family live in the Canadian Capital City of Ottawa.

SELECTED BOOKS BY THIS AUTHOR

1. *ZAMBIA: Struggles of My People (First and Second Editions)*
2. *10 FINANCIAL & WEALTH ATTITUDES TO AVOID*
3. *10 STRATEGIES TO DEFEAT STRESS AND DEPRESSION: Creating an Internal Safeguard against Stress and Depression*
4. *100+ REASONS TO READ BOOKS*
5. *A CASE FOR AFRICA?S LIBERTY: The Synergistic Transformation of Africa and the West into First-World Partnerships*
6. *DECOLONIZATION: Reclaiming African Originality and Destiny*
7. *A PANDEMIC POETRY, COVID-19*
8. *ALLERGIC TO CORRUPTION: The Legacy of President Michael Sata of Zambia*
9. *BOOK ABOUT SOMETHING: On Ultimate Purpose*
10. *CAMPAIGN FOR AFRICA: A Provocative Crusade for the Economic and Humanitarian Decolonization of Africa*
11. *CHAMPIONS: Application of Common Sense and Biblical Motifs to Succeed in Both*

15

Worlds
12. *FURGUSON FACTOR: Motivation, Strategy, Tactics*
13. *CORONAVIRUS PRAYERS*
14. *HH IS THE RIGHT MAN FOR ZAMBIA: And Other Acclaimed Articles on Zambia and Africa*
15. *I BOW: 3500 Prayer Lines of Inspiration & Intercession from the Heart: Volume One*
16. *INTERUNIVERSALISM IN A NUTSHELL: For Iranian Refugee Claimants*
17. *JURISPRUDENCE of GOOD AND RIGHT: A Treatise on Juridical Activism and Fiat*
18. *LAW & GRACE: An Expository Study in the Rudiments of Sin and Truth*
19. *LAWS OF INFLUENCE: 7even Lessons in Transformational Leadership*
20. *LOVE IDEAS IN COVID PANDEMIC TIMES: For Couples & Lovers*
21. *P.A.S.S: Version 2: Answer Bank*
22. *P.A.S.S.: Acing the Ontario Paralegal-Licensing Examination, Version 2*
23. *POETRY: The Best of Charles Mwewa*
24. *QUOT-EBOS: Essential. Barbs. Opinions. Sayings*

INDEX

| Z | 18 |

Zambia, 13, 15, 16, 17,